Social Studies Explorer

THAILAND

➡ by Lucia Raatma

CHERRY LAKE PUBLISHING • ANN ARBOR, MICHIGAN

Published in the United States of America
by Cherry Lake Publishing
Ann Arbor, Michigan
www.cherrylakepublishing.com

Content Adviser: Raymond Scuipin, PhD, Director, Center for International and Global
Studies and Department Chair, Anthropology and Sociology, Lindenwood University, St.
Charles, Missouri

Book design and production: The Design Lab

Photo credits: Cover, ©Dmitry Pichugin/Dreamstime.com; cover (stamp), ©Cpbackpacker/
Shutterstock, Inc.; page 4, ©Woraitp/Shutterstock, Inc.; page 5, ©Prawee Sriplakich/
Alamy; page 6, ©magicinfoto/Shutterstock, Inc.; page 8, ©Watperm/Shutterstock,
Inc.; page 9, ©Gusev Mikhail Evgenievich/Shutterstock, Inc.; page 10, ©Igor Prahin/
Shutterstock, Inc.; page 11, ©Tippawan Kunkeaw/Shutterstock, Inc.; pages 13 and
24, ©ASSOCIATED PRESS; page 14, ©Reinhold Leitner/Shutterstock, Inc.; page 15,
©Praisaeng/Shutterstock, Inc.; page 16, ©Ekkachai/Shutterstock, Inc.; page 17, ©Mohd
Yusof Tengku/Alamy; page 18, ©Gnomeandi/Alamy; page 19, ©PaulPaladin/Shutterstock,
Inc.; page 21, ©ZUMA Wire Service/Alamy; page 23, ©Presselect/Alamy; page 26, ©Hector
Conesa/Shutterstock, Inc.; page 27, ©imagebroker/Alamy; page 28, ©AA World Travel
Library/Alamy; page 31, ©LOOK Die Bildagentur der Fotografen GmbH/Alamy; page
33, ©Stuart Dee/Alamy; page 34, ©Rufous/Shutterstock, Inc.; page 37, ©photofriday/
Shutterstock, Inc.; page 38, ©Mai Techaphan/Shutterstock, Inc.; page 39, ©skyearth/
Shutterstock, Inc.; page 40, ©kiattisak chiphimai/Shutterstock, Inc.; page 41, ©Piyachok
Thawornmat/Shutterstock, Inc.; page 45, ©Charlie Edward/Shutterstock, Inc.

Library of Congress Cataloging-in-Publication Data
Raatma, Lucia.
  Thailand / by Lucia Raatma.
     p. cm.
  Includes bibliographical references and index.
  ISBN 978-1-61080-441-7 (lib. bdg.) — ISBN 978-1-61080-528-5 (e-book) —
ISBN 978-1-61080-615-2 (pbk.)
1. Thailand—Juvenile literature. I. Title.
  DS563.5.R33 2012
  959.3—dc23   2012001716

Cherry Lake Publishing would like to acknowledge the work of The Partnership for
21st Century Skills. Please visit www.21stcenturyskills.org for more information.

Printed in the United States of America
Corporate Graphics Inc.
July 2012
CLFA11

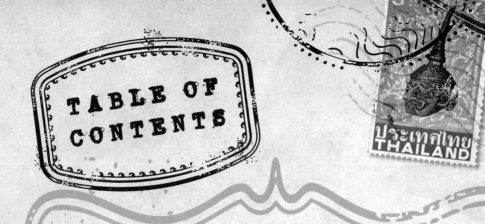

TABLE OF CONTENTS

CHAPTER ONE

WELCOME TO THAILAND!

➳ Huai Mae Khamin waterfall is just one example of Thailand's beautiful landscape.

Would you like to visit Thailand? This country is in Southeast Asia. It is the 50th-largest country in the world. It is a little larger than the state of California. Thailand is home to more than 67 million people. This land offers beautiful parks, amazing historical sites, and delicious food.

On your trip, you could explore the Grand Palace in the capital city of Bangkok. Or you could travel to Huai Mae Khamin waterfall. You could go rafting or hot air ballooning. You might also enjoy a day at the Dusit Zoo or at Siam Ocean World, the largest aquarium in Southeast Asia. No matter when you visit, you'll probably want to wear light clothing. However, during the rainy season, you should pack a poncho or an umbrella. Let's explore Thailand!

Visitors to Dusit Zoo can watch elephants paint pictures with their trunks.

The Grand Palace is a group of magnificent buildings in Bangkok. For many years, the palace was home to the Thai royal family. Today, it is used for special ceremonies and other important events.

Where in the world is Thailand? If you look at a globe, you'll see it on the continent of Asia. To the west is Myanmar. To the east are Laos and Cambodia. The Gulf of Thailand lies to the south. Part of Thailand also lies on the Malay **Peninsula**, and Malaysia is farther south.

Thailand extends 198,456 square miles (514,000 square kilometers). It is usually divided into four main regions: the central region, the northern region, the northeastern region, and the southern region.

The central region is sometimes called the Rice Bowl of Asia because its farmland is so rich. The rice grown there is sold to many other countries. The land is fed by the Chao Phraya River, which snakes through the region. You will also find the capital city of Bangkok there.

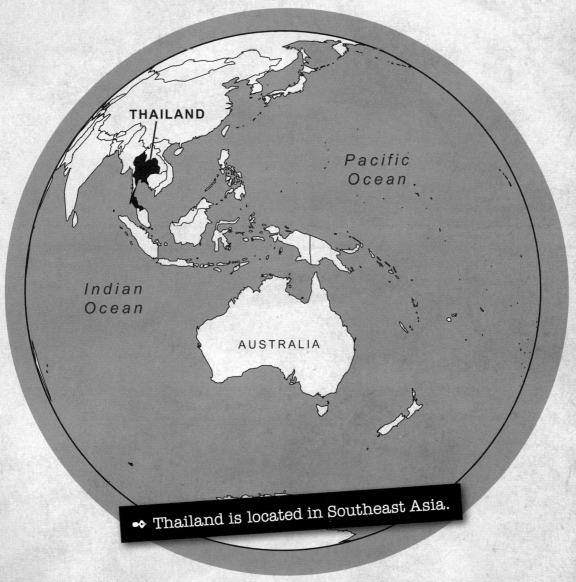

↪ Thailand is located in Southeast Asia.

The north boasts the largest forests in the country. Mount Inthanon is located in this region. At 8,481 feet (2,585 meters), it is the highest peak in Thailand. Many people enjoy climbing the area's mountains.

In the northeastern region is the Khorat **Plateau**. This area is home to small hills and lakes. People raise horses, cattle, and pigs on the plateau. Farmers grow

crops such as cotton, corn, rice, and peanuts. Many tourists enjoy swimming in the Mekong River, which is also in this region. The river offers a beautiful view of towns such as Nong Khai and Mukdahan.

The south includes the area on the Malay Peninsula. Tourists come to explore this region's islands, including Phuket, Ko Samui, Ko Pha Ngan, and Ko Tao. People also appreciate the beautiful beaches here. If you visit, you might try kayaking, scuba diving, or fishing. This region is also known for growing rubber plants.

Tourists come to Phuket and other Thai islands to enjoy warm weather and relax on beaches.

Bangkok is the biggest city in Thailand. This city and surrounding areas are home to 9.3 million people. You will find many banks and other financial businesses there. You may enjoy visiting museums, such as the National Gallery of Thailand and the Bangkok Art and Culture Centre. Other big cities include Nakhon

❖ Bangkok is a huge, sprawling city.

❧ Pattaya's coastal location makes it a popular tourist destination.

Ratchasima in the northeast, Pak Kret in the central region, and Hat Yai near the Malaysian border. Pattaya, located on the Gulf of Thailand, is a beautiful coastal town. It boasts Asia's biggest beachfront shopping mall.

Another important place is Chiang Mai, a historical city in the north. It has beautiful temples and statues. Hua Hin in the central region is likely the oldest beach resort in the country.

ACTIVITY

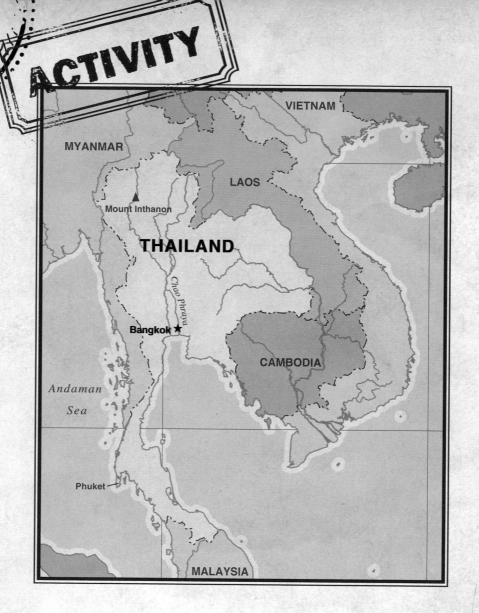

Practice your skills as a mapmaker. Look at the map of Thailand above. Place a piece of paper over the map and trace the outline of the country. See where Bangkok is? Mark that city with a star on your tracing. Also label the island of Phuket and Mount Inthanon. Now, label the Chao Phraya River. Do you see how part of Thailand extends south on the peninsula? Notice the other countries that border Thailand.

On December 26, 2004, Thailand was hit by a devastating **tsunami**. It began with an earthquake in the Indian Ocean that created a huge wave. The tsunami hit the beaches of Thailand without warning. On that day, as many as 8,000 people died in Thailand. Towns were damaged or destroyed. In the years since, many of the towns have rebuilt, and tourists are visiting again.

Different areas in Thailand have different weather. In the central, northern, and northeastern regions, there are three seasons. From June to October is the rainy season, which is typically hot, wet, and humid. From November to February, the weather is cooler. From March to May, the weather is usually hot and sunny. Temperatures range from as low as 50 degrees Fahrenheit (10 degrees Celsius) to as high as 100°F

(38°C). The average yearly rainfall for these regions is nearly 500 inches (1,270 centimeters).

The southern region has a completely different climate. Its weather is similar to a tropical rain forest. Rain can be expected year-round, and the average temperature is 82°F (28°C).

➥ The white-handed gibbon eats mostly fruit and leaves.

➥ Despite its nickname, the bear cat is neither a bear nor a cat.

You can find many different animals in Thailand. The country has 285 species of mammals and 925 species of birds. Some of these animals live in protected areas, such as Khao Yai National Park.

The white-handed gibbon can be found in Thai jungles. It is known for singing at each sunrise. It also sings to mark its territory and to attract mates. Binturongs, also called bear cats, come out mostly at night. They

One of Thailand's **endangered** species is the Asian elephant. This huge creature can weigh up to 12,000 pounds (5,443 kilograms). It lives mostly in forests and mountains, where it feeds on bark, twigs, grasses, and leaves. Hundreds of years ago, elephants played a big role in transportation. They carried people and supplies from place to place. Today, some elephants are in danger because the natural area they live in has been destroyed. Others have been killed by farmers trying to protect their crops.

have amazing tails that help them balance as they rest in trees. Dusky langurs, also called leaf monkeys, live in large groups in Thailand's forests.

The purple swamphen lives in marshes and lakes. This bird has a loud screech and is a good swimmer. It feeds on fish and snails. Another interesting animal is

the bubble crab. This tiny creature is only about as big as a person's fingernail. It burrows on Thai beaches and lives off the nutrients found in sand.

Thailand's natural areas are breathtaking. Many people visit to explore its parks, lakes, and mountains. Does that sound exciting to you?

❖ Because of its size and color, the bubble crab can be difficult to spot in the wild.

CHAPTER TWO

BUSINESS AND GOVERNMENT IN THAILAND

☛ Rice farms are a common sight in many parts of Thailand.

People have been living in what is now Thailand for thousands of years. The Tai were a group of people who lived in China and moved to this area. For a long time,

The baht is the form of money in Thailand. Each baht is divided into 100 satang. Satang are coins made of aluminum and other metals. Baht can be banknotes or coins. The banknotes are very colorful. Different monetary amounts are green, blue, red, purple, and brown. In June 2012, one U.S. dollar equaled 31.72 baht.

the area was called Siam. Its name officially became Thailand in the 1930s. Over time, Thailand has grown and changed.

For many years, most people in Thailand relied on farming to make a living. Even today, Thailand exports more rice than any other country. It sends rice to Iran, Nigeria, the United States, China, Hong Kong, South Africa, and other places all over the world. Thailand also exports rubber, pineapples, seafood, tin, and other materials.

Thailand imports and exports goods with other countries. Good relationships with other countries help make this trading system work. Here are some of Thailand's most important import and export partners.

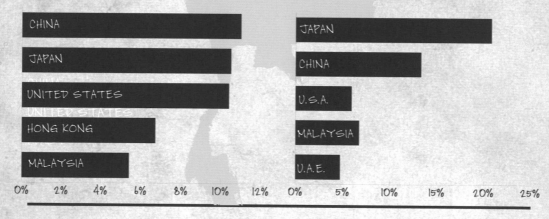

IMPORTS ⟶ THAILAND ⟶ EXPORTS

IMPORTS		EXPORTS	
CHINA		JAPAN	
JAPAN		CHINA	
UNITED STATES		U.S.A.	
HONG KONG		MALAYSIA	
MALAYSIA		U.A.E.	

Imports axis: 0% 2% 4% 6% 8% 10% 12%
Exports axis: 0% 5% 10% 15% 20% 25%

In recent years, Thailand has started manufacturing goods such as clothing and electronics. Many automotive parts are manufactured in Thailand. Check a laser printer or DVD player. It might have been made in Thailand. You might have a shirt or bag from Thailand, too.

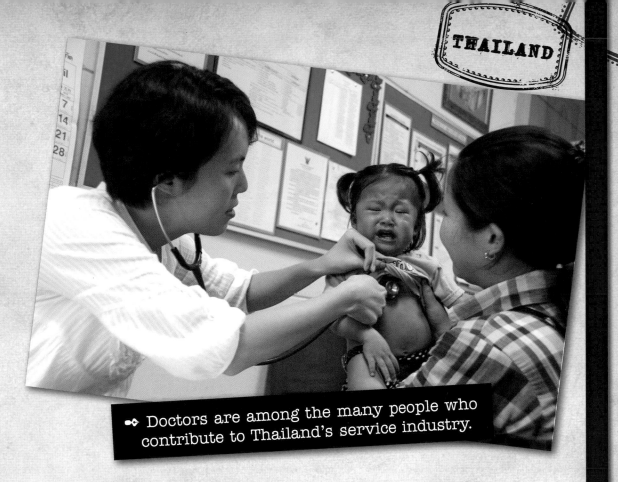

●◆ Doctors are among the many people who contribute to Thailand's service industry.

Another important part of Thailand's **economy** is the service industry. Service workers include doctors, teachers, and bank managers. Tourism is very important in Thailand. People from all over the world visit the beaches and historical sites. Hotel workers, restaurant owners, and shopkeepers are all service workers who help support tourism.

Thailand's government is a constitutional **monarchy**. Its leader is a monarch who follows the guidelines of a **constitution**. A monarch is not elected, but belongs to a royal family and is born into the position. Thailand has had 17 constitutions. The most recent one was adopted in 2007.

ACTIVITY

As of 2008, about 42 percent of people in Thailand worked in the agriculture industry. Another 38 percent worked in the service industry and 20 percent in manufacturing.

Based on this information, create a bar graph that shows these main parts of Thailand's economy. Ask an adult for help if you need it. Label the horizontal axis "Type of Industry." Label the vertical axis "Percentage of Thai Workers." Also label each bar with the type of industry. Which bar is the shortest? Which is the longest?

STOP
Don't write in this book!

King Bhumibol Adulyadej is Thailand's current monarch. Born in 1927, he has been on the throne since 1946. This makes him the longest reigning monarch in the world.

The governing body of Thailand is the National Assembly. It includes two houses: the House of Representatives and the Senate. Members of both houses are elected to office. Both the House and the Senate meet at the Parliament House of Thailand.

The Council of Ministers leads Thailand's many departments. Among them are the Ministry of Finance, the Ministry of Education, and the Ministry of Public Health. The prime minister, who is elected to office, leads the council.

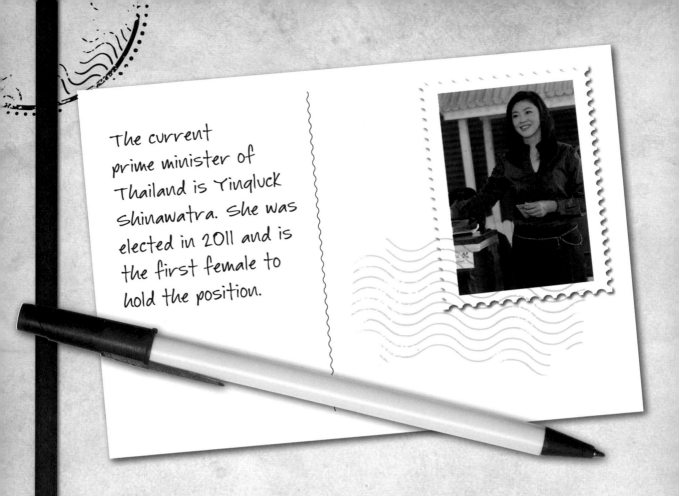

The current prime minister of Thailand is Yingluck Shinawatra. She was elected in 2011 and is the first female to hold the position.

In Thailand, the court system has three parts. They are the Administrative Courts, the Constitutional Court, and the Courts of Justice. The Administrative Courts try cases between private citizens and the government. The Constitutional Court decides whether laws are in line with Thailand's constitution. The Courts of Justice oversee all other cases. Over the years, the court system has been criticized as being unfair. It is reported that people are put on trial without evidence of crime. Accused people can wait years for their trial to begin. Punishment for crimes in Thailand can be very harsh. For example,

people can receive life sentences in jail for using and selling drugs. Citizens can also go to prison for insulting the king or queen.

Thailand is divided into 76 provinces called *changwat*. Cities such as Bangkok, Pattaya, and Chiang Mai have fairly powerful local governments. Their leaders are often elected to the National Assembly. Villages also have local governments. They elect leaders called *muban*. In both small villages and big cities, people work hard to lead happy and successful lives. Let's learn more about the people of Thailand.

The Thai flag was adopted in 1917. It has five horizontal stripes of red, white, and blue. The middle blue stripe is twice as wide as the red and white stripes.

CHAPTER THREE

MEET THE PEOPLE

The people of Thailand live in both large cities and small towns.

When you think of Thailand, do you think of busy cities with tall buildings? Or do you imagine quiet mountain villages? Thailand has both! It also has small towns and seaside communities. As of 2010, about 34 percent of

Thai people live in **urban** areas, while 66 percent live in **rural** areas.

Most people in Thailand are Thai. They are **descendants** of people who have lived in the area since the 1200s. Thailand is also home to people from China, Malaysia, and other areas. The Mon-Khmer people live primarily in northern Thailand. They are closely related to the Khmer people of neighboring Cambodia.

Thailand's official language is Thai, and most people speak it. However, the language has many forms, or

➥ The Thai language uses its own unique alphabet.

dialects. Different dialects are used for everyday communication, formal communication, religion, royalty, and public speaking. Other languages include Mon-Khmer and Austronesian, a form of a Malaysian language. Most people in southern Thailand speak Malay. Many people also speak English, which is a required language course in most schools. English is often used in government and business.

➥ It is not uncommon to see signs in both Thai and English in many parts of Thailand.

THAI

Let's learn some Thai words and phrases. Look at the lists below. You'll see the English phrase, the Thai phrase, and the Thai pronunciation. Practice saying these words, and try them out with your friends!

ENGLISH	THAI	PRONUNCIATION
Thank you	Kòp Kun	Kop-KUHN
Hello	sà-wàt-dee	sah-wat-DEE
Good-bye	laa gòn ná	lah gohn NAH
Excuse me	Kŏr tôht	Kaw TOHT
Help!	chûay dûay!	choo-WAY doo-WAY

When you see Thai words, they may be written using the alphabet you know. However, Thai is traditionally written with a different alphabet. The symbols represent 44 consonants and various vowels. Sentences are written left to right with no spaces. Thai is a tonal language. The meanings of many words depend on how they are pronounced.

In Thailand, most people follow a system called **hierarchy**. Relationships are defined by who is superior. For instance, parents are seen as superior to their children. Bosses are superior to their workers. Teachers are

The Thai alphabet is very pretty. This is what "good luck" looks like:

ขอให้โชคดี

superior to their students. Thai children are taught to honor and respect their elders and other superiors.

You will often see Thai people greet one another with a *wai*. This is a gesture in which a person joins his hands palm to palm and touches them to his forehead or chest.

Children are guaranteed 12 years of free education. They are required to go to school for at least nine years. However, many children in rural areas do not complete all these years. Their families need them to work on

farms. Still, more than 90 percent of Thai people can read and write.

Thailand has dozens of fine colleges and universities. Some of the most respected are Chulalongkorn University, Thammasat University, and Kasetsart University in Bangkok. There is also the Asian Institute of Technology in Pathum Thani.

Nearly 95 percent of the people in Thailand practice a form of the Buddhist religion called Theravada

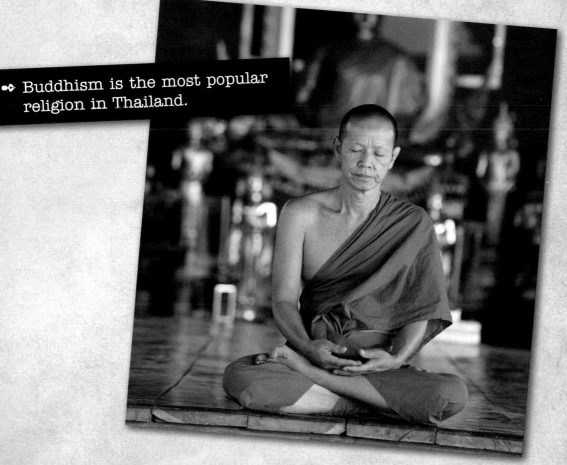

↜ Buddhism is the most popular religion in Thailand.

Buddha is the name given to Siddhartha Gautama (ca. 563 BCE–ca. 483 BCE), a spiritual teacher from India. His teachings formed the basis of Buddhism. Today, you can see many statues of Buddha throughout Thailand.

Buddhism. Other religions in Thailand include Islam and Christianity. Theravada Buddhism often includes Thai traditions of respecting ancestors and the spirit world. Most Buddhist families have spirit houses near their homes. These are small structures where spirits are believed to live. Buddhists often leave fruit, nuts, and other offerings to the spirits. In many towns, the neighborhood Buddhist temple—called a *wat*—is the center of the community.

Much of the art in Thailand is related to Buddhism. Throughout the country, you will likely see many

religious paintings and statues. In the temples, you may see beautiful murals with religious themes. Thai artists are also known for their jewelry, glass mosaics, ceramics, and wood carvings.

From the big cities to the small villages, the people of Thailand appreciate beauty, both inside and out. They make their surroundings appealing, but they also try to be kind and courteous to one another.

❖ Beautiful Thai murals often tell religious or historical stories.

CHAPTER FOUR

CELEBRATIONS!

Thai kites come in all sorts of incredible shapes.

An important ideal in Thailand is *sanuk*. This is the belief that life should be fun. Often, sanuk means spending time with family and friends.

If you're in Thailand between March and May, look to the skies! Kite flying, known as *len wow*, is very popular during these warm months. This tradition dates back to the 1200s.

MAKE A THAI KITE

When people in Thailand make kites, some are for flying and some are for decoration. Try this activity to create a kite that can decorate your room.

MATERIALS

- Long rectangular piece of watercolor paper
- Glue
- Crayons
- Newspaper
- Watercolor paint
- Paintbrushes
- Scissors
- Ribbon
- Fabric scraps

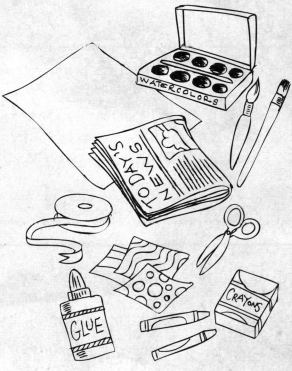

INSTRUCTIONS

1. Lay the watercolor paper flat. Fold the top two corners about one-quarter of the way down. Then fold the bottom two corners about three-quarters up. This should create a long diamond shape. Glue the folds and allow the glue to dry.

2. Flip the sheet over so the glued folds are on the back. Using crayons, draw a design on the side that now faces up. You could try drawing birds, flowers, or bright shapes.

3. Spread newspaper over a work area. Lay your diamond-shaped sheet on top. Using watercolor paint and brushes, paint over your crayon design. No need to paint inside the lines! The wax in the crayon will resist the paint, and your design will come through. After you finish painting, allow the sheet to dry.

4. For the kite's tail, cut a strip of ribbon as long as you like. Cut fabric scraps and glue them to the ribbon to make a colorful pattern. Now glue the tail to the bottom of your kite.

5. Try making lots of different kites for your wall!

➟ Muay Thai is an exciting form of kickboxing.

Thailand's most popular sport is football, called soccer in the United States. In 2007, Thailand joined three other countries in hosting the Asian Cup football tournament.

Many people enjoy watching muay Thai, which is Thai kickboxing. Kraabi Krabong is a martial art that uses swords, sticks, and poles. Have you ever heard of sepak takraw? This game is similar to volleyball, but

The Phuket King's Cup **Regatta** is held every December. It is the biggest regatta in all of Asia. It began in 1987 to honor the 60th birthday of His Majesty King Bhumibol Adulyadej.

instead of using their hands, players use their feet! Thailand's miles of coastline make boating very popular, too. People enjoy sailing, canoeing, and yachting.

The people of Thailand get to celebrate three separate New Years. The first is January 1, which is New Year's Day for much of the world. The second is Chinese New Year, usually in January or February. The third is the Songkran Festival. This is the Thai new year, and the country's most important holiday. It is celebrated from April 13 to April 15.

Another important holiday is Chakri Memorial Day on April 6. It remembers the beginning of the Chakri **Dynasty**, Thailand's current royal family. The holiday also honors the founding of Bangkok in 1782.

These are some of the national holidays recognized in Thailand:

January 1	New Year's Day
April 6	Chakri Memorial Day
April 13–15	Songkran Festival
May 5	Coronation Day
December 10	Constitution Day

CHAPTER FIVE

WHAT'S FOR DINNER?

➥ Many Thai dishes are served over rice.

Have you ever been to a Thai restaurant? Thai food is often very spicy. Cooks balance that spiciness with sweet, salty, and sour flavors.

One key ingredient for any Thai dish is rice. Thai food also uses noodles as a base. Meals can feature tofu,

meat, and fish. Curries are popular dishes made with coconut milk, garlic, and various seasonings. Fish sauce is in almost all Thai recipes. Another key ingredient is shrimp paste, which is made of ground shrimp and salt.

Thai cooking relies heavily on fresh vegetables, herbs, and spices. Many recipes call for eggplant, kale, corn, beans, bean sprouts, cabbage, and sweet potatoes.

Pad Thai is one of the best-known Thai dishes. It is often made with rice, chicken or shrimp, noodles, and bean sprouts. It's tossed in a sauce that includes fish sauce and

Every Thai cook has his or her own version of pad Thai.

The durian is a unique-looking fruit. It is large, with a thorn-covered husk. Called the King of fruits, the durian has a strong smell that few people like. Most people find it overwhelming!

palm sugar. Throughout Thailand, cooks offer various versions of pad Thai, and they are probably all delicious!

Fruit is usually served after meals. Popular fruits include pineapple, mango, papaya, and durian.

For breakfast, many people eat rice porridge or rice soup. Common drinks include tea and coffee. Krating Daeng is an energy drink that originated in Thailand. It contains caffeine, sugar, and vitamins. Today's popular energy drink Red Bull is based on Krating Daeng.

There are lots of different Thai foods to try. Here is an easy recipe to start with. Be sure to have an adult nearby to help. Experiment with this soup and add other vegetables if you like!

Thai Vegetarian Soup

INGREDIENTS
1 tablespoon vegetable oil
2 cloves garlic, sliced
3 cups broccoli, chopped
2 small carrots, sliced
1 inch fresh gingerroot
3 scallions, chopped
2 tablespoons lemongrass, chopped
2 cups mushrooms, sliced
32 ounces vegetable broth
2 tablespoons red curry paste
Salt and pepper, to taste

INSTRUCTIONS

1. Heat oil in a saucepan over medium-high heat. Add garlic and stir until garlic is brown.
2. Add broccoli and carrots and stir-fry until slightly tender. Remove broccoli and carrots and set aside.
3. Add ginger, scallions, and lemongrass to saucepan and stir-fry for 2 minutes.
4. Add mushrooms and stir-fry for another 2 minutes.
5. Add vegetable broth and red curry paste. Add salt and pepper as desired. Bring to a boil.
6. Reduce to a simmer and heat, covered, for 5 minutes.
7. Uncover and add the broccoli and carrots. Heat for another minute or two.
8. Remove from heat. Spoon into bowls. This is great served with rice.

↝ You'll have plenty of opportunities to eat delicious foods and see incredible sights if you visit Thailand.

Families often take time to cook a meal and eat it together. Whether they live in a small village or a Bangkok apartment, sharing food is important. Do you like to share food with your family and friends?

Be sure to keep reading books and exploring Web sites about Thailand. Maybe one day you will visit Thailand in person!

GLOSSARY

constitution (kon-sti-TOO-shun) a document that sets up a government system

descendants (di-SEN-duhnts) members of a person's family who live after him

dynasty (DYE-nuh-stee) a series of rulers who belong to the same family

economy (i-KON-uh-mee) the system in which a country runs its industry, trade, and finances

endangered (en-DAYN-jurd) at risk of dying out

hierarchy (HIRE-ar-kee) a system in which people or things are organized by importance

monarch (MON-ark) a ruler, such as a king or queen, who is born into the position

peninsula (puh-NIN-suh-luh) an area of land that sticks out from a larger landmass and is almost completely surrounded by water

plateau (pla-TOH) an area of high, flat land

regatta (ri-GAT-uh) a boat race or a group of boat races

rural (RUR-uhl) having to do with the country or farming

tsunami (tsoo-NAH-mee) a very large, destructive wave caused by an underwater earthquake or volcano

urban (UR-buhn) having to do with cities

THAILAND

FOR MORE INFORMATION

Books

Cunningham, Kevin. *Surviving Tsunamis*. Chicago: Heinemann-Raintree, 2012.

Donaldson, Madeline. *Thailand*. Minneapolis: Lerner Publishing Group, 2012.

Hawker, Frances, and Sunantha Phusomsai. *Buddhism in Thailand*. New York: Crabtree Publishing, 2009.

Kummer, Patricia K. *The Food of Thailand*. New York: Marshall Cavendish Benchmark, 2012.

Web Sites

Central Intelligence Agency: The World Factbook—Thailand
https://www.cia.gov/library/publications/the-world-factbook/geos/th.html
Check out this site for information about Thailand's economy, geography, population, and government.

The Senate of Thailand
www.senate.go.th/th_senate/English/index.htm
Learn more about Thailand's government at this site.

Tourism Authority of Thailand
www.tourismthailand.org
This site offers city-by-city information about attractions, festivals, and historical places to visit.

INDEX

ABOUT THE AUTHOR
Lucia Raatma has written dozens of books for young readers. Her favorite Thai dish is sautéed vegetables with rice and tofu. She and her family live in the Tampa Bay area of Florida.